Inspirational Spoken Word

I KNOW HOW I LOOK NOW ... BUT KEEP WATCHING

Inspired by Cece Peterson

Written by: D.Y. Myrick

I KNOW HOW I LOOK NOW... BUT
KEEP WATCHING
Copyright © 2020 Denise Myrick

Disclaimer
Quotes which do not have author names are not
original to this book author, rather, they are from
the Being Mary Jane quote wall.

Illustration by Michael E. Grandison, Jr.

DEDICATION

This book is dedicated to my Royal Grands, Princess Skyy, Lady McKenzie and Prince Charming (Tristen).

They have shown such resilience during the death of their mother and the relocation from all that they knew to a place where nothing and no one was familiar but me.

Their love and strength is the reason I began this book.

G-ma loves you guys!!!

TABLE OF CONTENT

INTRODUCTION

My daughter, Chalan V. Peterson, widely known
as Cece, was a loyal, fiery, vibrant woman.
She transitioned at the age of 29 years old,
on the Dan Ryan Expressway in Chicago, IL,
the day after Thanksgiving, 2015.
She left behind three beautiful, intelligent
children. She also left behind a few
journals. Yes, she liked to club, drink and
dance. She also would curse and fight. Her
temper was WHOA!!! However, Cece was a loyal
mother and friend. If she was in your corner,
it didn't matter the circumstances, you could
count on her having your back. She was great
with her babies and laid a firm foundation
for them. My daughter's finished work was her
three babies. Regardless of the tragedy that
they have suffered, just wait and watch to
see what she poured into them. Most of these
are passages inspired by entries that were
retrieved from my daughter's journals. It is
my hope that this book inspires women as well
as men to push beyond what the present
situation looks like and press towards what
your future can be.
I used to tell my Baby, "If you give it your
best and that's not good enough then make
your best better. Add an A game to your best
game!!!"

FOREWORD

I Know How I Look Now, but... Keep Watching reminds us that the journey of life is about purpose, movement and discovery. Sometimes, we plant our feet in the wrong places of pain, despair, and disappointment. We dwell in those places and spaces that were never intended to keep us but teach us a lesson that would prepare us for our next.

The cultivation of each piece is a reflection of a mother's love. Denise does a wonderful job of sharing her daughter's heart during her moments of realization and transformation. These words of truth speak to our positions and postures as we are challenged to examine our thoughts, realize who and whose we are and commit to becoming.

No matter where you are on your journey, you can grow, you can rise, you can become... you can push through.

The joy of your tomorrow may be determined by the strength of your today.

Push!

Alicia L. Waters
Author of "A Word For Your Womb: A Collection of Psalms, Prayers, Poetry & Praise"

"

**A REAL MOM:
EMOTIONAL YET THE ROCK,
TIRED BUT KEEPS GOING,
WORRIED BUT FULL OF HOPE,
IMPATIENT BUT STILL PATIENT,
OVERWHELMED BUT NEVER QUITS.
AMAZING EVEN THOUGH DOUBTED.
WONDERFUL EVEN IN THE CHAOS.
LIFE CHANGER EVERY SINGLE DAY.**

Rachel Martin

"

I'M A MOTHER FOR REAL

Yeah I'm a millennial Mom!
I like to kick it,
I club and hang out,
But before ALL that, I'm a
Mother.
My dude doesn't get more from
me than my Babies do,
I'll look like a bum so my
Babies can look fresh.
I cook, do their hair, and
help with homework... I even do
flash cards to help build
their vocabulary.
The streets don't come before
my Babies.
Some broads have their hair
done, nails done, new outfit,
out at the club and there
ain't no toilet tissue or
toothpaste at the house.
Yeah, I'm a young mother... but
I'm a Mother for **REAL**!!!

EVERYONE COMES WITH BAGGAGE...

FIND SOMEONE WHO LOVES YOU ENOUGH TO HELP YOU UNPACK.

A GLAM SQUAD

It's important to have a crew in your corner that elevates you. People who enhance your skills; A Glam Squad.
They make you more beautiful than you already are. A Glam Squad is what a song artist or actress has before they go on stage or a movie set.
Have you ever seen Oprah without makeup??? She has a Glam Squad. People need a Glam Squad to be productive in life. We need to align ourselves with people that put a demand on our hidden potential. A Glam Squad makes you better. A Glam Squad brings out the best in you.

Say you write inspirational notes on social media everyday, your Glam Squad encourages you to consider writing a book.

Say you are good at braiding your children's hair, Your Glam Squad gets you some people that will pay you to braid hair.

Look, you need to evaluate your crew and if they are not Glam Squad material, you need to get a new crew.

You need a Glam Squad in your life

THINK DIFFERENT

Steve Jobs

I CAN'T SEE FOR LOOKING

It's really funny when you think about it...
I'm so busy thinking that I'm looking for
the silver lining, the good part, the
breakthrough, the "it's all good" but in
reality, all I'm looking at is the negative
stuff and thinking about the "what ifs"
until I totally miss the greatness that GOD
has given me.
Sure, I don't have the kind of money I
would like to have, which means I don't
have a lot of things that I would like to
buy, but what about what I do have?

Like I'm healthy, my two Babies are healthy
and smart, We live in a good environment in
Chicago, I have two cars and I'm only 25
years old and all my basic needs are met.

Some of my friends can't say that. I really
had to take the blinders off and be
thankful for my blessings.

I really couldn't see for looking...

I'm straight now though. I'm covered and
just acting spoiled as we all sometimes do.

Look at the good instead of the negatives,
then you'll be able to see what you weren't
looking at.

I WAS GRATIFIED TO BE ABLE TO ANSWER PROMPTLY, AND I DID. I SAID I DIDN'T KNOW.

Mark Twain

DO YOU KNOW WHAT I DON'T KNOW?

I enjoy my friends and I'm comfortable around them.

Yet, lately, I've been thinking that I need to be uncomfortable.

Maybe I need to be around people that are on a different level than me.

I might need a new type of environment. Maybe I need to be around people that know more than me and different things than me.

I mean... how will I grow and advance if I stay with people who are on the same level as I am?

I think I need to get with some people who know stuff that I don't know.

" "

THERE IS NOTHING MORE CLASSY AND POWERFUL THAN SHOWING FORGIVENESS AND GRACE TO SOMEONE WHO DOES NOT DESERVE IT

" "

EMOTIONAL PAIN

Emotional pain is a MONSTER, and if you let her hang around too long, she will mess you up.

The problem with emotional pain is there is no easy way to get rid of her fast and the longer she lives in you, the more damage she causes.

I wish there was a recipe to remove emotional pain when she first arrives, however, there isn't.

What worked for me was prayer, after realizing that beating myself up wasn't working and being angry and mean all the time wasn't helping.

Prayer eased my emotional pain until she was no longer mine.

NO BEAUTY SHINES BRIGHTER THAN THAT OF A GOOD HEART.

Kushandwizdom

WE ARE DIAMONDS

I'm the Prize.

I'm a Woman.

GOD created me as a gift to man.

Every human on earth is birthed from a Woman.

We are like an exquisite diamond set on plush black velvet.

Exquisite Diamonds are not seen on commercials and they are never on sale.

Stop begging for attention Ladies!!!

We are Diamonds, so be an EXQUISITE DIAMOND and stop acting like a cubic zirconia.

IT'S IRONIC HOW WE OFTEN FORGET THE THINGS WORTH REMEMBERING, BUT REMEMBER THE THINGS WORTH FORGETTING.

iliketoquote.com

YOU FORGOT

America, you forgot that this country was built on the backs of Black people.

You really forgot that Black Women were the foundation because everyone comes here through the womb of a woman.

America, you forgot that Black women maintained your households, we cooked for your families and cleaned your homes and gave birth to your children because you raped us.

Your wives weren't cooking, we were…
You forgot.

America you forgot that we were the mammies to your children so they could grow up and continue the oppression that you all started.

You forgot that most Black households are headed by women.

America, you forgot that although some of us may not make a lot of money yet without our money, this country's economy would collapse.

You forgot that Black women's money is a large percentage of what buys Happy Meals, Jordans, Apple products and keeps Amazon busy to name a few.

America, you forgot that BLACK WOMEN'S LIVES MATTER!!!

YOU FORGOT

Inspired by the murders of: Sandra Bland & Breonna Taylor along with countless others.

"

DON'T BLAME A CLOWN FOR
ACTING LIKE A CLOWN.
BLAME YOURSELF FOR GOING
TO THE CIRCUS.

"

EVICTION

Say you spent 10-20 million dollars on a Learjet, would you let someone else fly and control the schedule of your jet the majority of the time without charging them??? Of course not!!! So why do you allow people/things to live rent free in your mind? They live there and serve no purpose but to irritate and distract you. They are the same as a tenant who hasn't paid rent in months, yet will not move out without you going through the eviction process.

This thing called life is over sooner than you think. You don't have time to let people/things that serve no healthy purpose in your life to dominate space in your mind. You need to serve them an eviction notice and rid yourself of unproductive people and things. Sure, there are some things that are more difficult to evict than others, just like with tenants. However, those things can be turned over to GOD so that you can stop worrying and just trust him to handle it. This is almost like hiring a property manager to handle your rental property. The manager gets paid to handle the problem which takes the burden off of you.

Ok… it's time to take inventory and start the eviction process so that you can be the best you possible!

"

**DEAR LORD,
INTO YOUR HANDS I PLACE MY
WORRIES. INTO YOUR WISDOM
I PLACE MY PATH, DIRECTION,
AND MY GOAL.
INTO YOUR LOVE I PLACE MY
LIFE**

"

DOES PRAYER REALLY WORK

You know, I watched my Mom pray but a lot of times, I didn't see a change in the situation. For a while, it just looked like a waste of time and energy.

It's funny though because life has a way of bringing things home to you. The Lord really has a way of helping you out when you are confused or doubtful about him and most times, it's not in a nice way.
Let me tell you, he placed somethings in my path that made me try prayer because nothing else was working.

What I found out was that even if it didn't look like the situation was changing, I was changing how I handled that thing. It wasn't as hard to deal with anymore. Prayer is like internal reconstruction. Your whole way of looking at the situation changes which makes it easier. It's like finding the missing piece to a puzzle. Then sometimes, the Lord will just answer your prayer just like you asked. Now I have to warn you, that doesn't happen a lot but even when it doesn't happen like that, down the road you understand why. It may sound crazy but I'm glad that I reached a place in life where I was forced to pray because I was able to find out that prayer really does work!

A WOMAN WHO CATCHES A MAN'S EYE EARNS A PURSE, A WOMAN THAT CAPTURES HIS HEART EARNS HIS WORLD.

Chris Brew

I LIKE FRUIT LOOPS

Ladies, when a guy tells you that his favorite cereal is fruit loops, take him at his word.

The fact that when he comes to your place, he eats frosted flakes (because that's all you buy), does not mean that he has changed his mind about his favorite cereal. He is just consuming what is available to him.

We as women think we can change a man's mindset just because he keeps coming back for more. It's cereal and it's available; it's just not his favorite.

So if a man tells you he doesn't want commitment, stop trying to change his mind, then get upset when you find out there is someone else. He told you his favorite cereal was **FRUIT LOOPS**

THE MOST TERRIFYING THING IS TO ACCEPT ONE'S SELF COMPLETELY.

C.G Jung

I DON'T WANT TO

There are some days that I just don't want to...

I don't want to get my Babies ready for school, I don't want to go to work, I don't want to fix dinner, I don't want to talk on the phone, text, or even get on social media.

There are days when I just want to do me… whatever it is that me wants to do that day.

BUT if I'm teaching my Babies to be consistent and responsible, then I have to do the same.

Don't get me wrong, it's a push to do it, yet I know it will pay off in the end. Every now and then, I give into that selfish side of me, that "I don't want to" phase and it feels good, however, I know that I have to stay on track if I want my Babies to be better than me because...

I DON'T WANT TO FAIL MY BABIES!

YOU, YOURSELF AS MUCH AS ANYONE IN THE ENTIRE UNIVERSE DESERVE YOUR LOVE AND AFFECTION

Gautama Buddha

I CAN'T BE 2ND

I'm nobody's side chick.

I don't know how to be 2nd. I require too much attention. So, how did I end up falling for a guy that lived with a woman?

Did I really not see the signs or was I too busy enjoying the time we spent?
WOW it hurt so bad to let go but I just can't be 2nd.

The pain was so bad because I loved him. I even tried for a week to knowingly share but it's just not how I'm built.

So I got myself together, worked through the pain, and didn't settle for 2nd when I'm made to be the one and ONLY.

YOU CANNOT JUDGE PEOPLE BECAUSE THEY SIN DIFFERENTLY THAN YOU.

Erykah Badu

NO BURNT BRIDGES

My grandma taught me that you never know who you are going to have to turn to before you leave this earth.

I took that to mean no burnt bridges. Well just let me tell you, sometimes that's hard, especially with the people I'm around. I've had some stuff happen in my life that reminded me of what my grandma said. Fortunately, the bridges weren't burnt, just damaged, and my friends and I were able to repair it together.

Listen to me good, NEVER let disagreements or arguments outweigh the good in a relationship. You never know if the good in the relationship may be needed later in life.

If you have some damaged bridges, start the repair work. Work on having a NO burnt bridges motto for your life.

"

A PERSON'S ACTIONS WILL TELL YOU EVERYTHING YOU NEED TO KNOW.

"

KNOW WHO'S WHO.

Friends...
Man there are really levels of friendship
and at times, I have to keep these
categories in perspective in my own mind.
There are the Club friends - we kick it and
have a good time.
Then there are the friends that I can talk
to about some things but not things close
to my heart... and let me tell you I have
quite a few of these two levels of friends.

It's the ride or die friends that are hard
to find. I say it all the time, don't be
quick to call somebody your friend until
you know who's who because if you haven't
been through some mess with a person and
been able to recover from it and still love
each other, then that person is not a ride
or die friend.

You've got to be able to push past the
hardships to be considered a true friend.

Friends are with you when you are right and
wrong; they just check you later, when it's
just the two of you, about your wrongs.

NEVER NEVER NEVER GIVE UP!

Winston Churchill

THE 11th HOUR

Do you ever feel like you are always being tested on how much you can take before you just lose it?

Then the interesting part is right when you are at the point where you can't take even one more thing, the breakthrough comes…

Right at the 11th hour

Why do I have to almost get to the breaking point before I get relief???

Is there something I'm supposed to be gaining from all the stress that really could've been avoided if the breakthrough had come in the 2nd hour or at least the 5th hour?

Does this keep happening because I'm missing some key piece so I have to repeat this process in various circumstances of life?

Am I supposed to just ride it out and assume that the breakthrough will always come at the 11th hour?

Suppose it doesn't come and I lose my mind from stress.

Seriously, I need some help understanding why I have to be on this 11th hour cycle.

I sure would like to see what it feels like to get relief from the issues of life in the 2nd, 3rd, or even 7th

hour, WOULDN'T YOU???

WORRY ABOUT YOUR CHARACTER AND NOT YOUR REPUTATION, BECAUSE YOUR CHARACTER IS WHO YOU ARE AND YOUR REPUTATION IS ONLY WHAT PEOPLE THINK OF YOU.

Picsandquotes.com

A BECOMER

Are you a becomer?
Are you enhancing your hidden abilities?
Are you pushing past the pain to achieve your goals?

Are you a becomer?
Are you better this year than you were last year?
Are you striving for things that may seem unattainable?

Are you a
becomer?
Are you resting in what you have already achieved?
Are you satisfied?

You should always excel as long as you are alive.
You should always move to new levels.

BECOME A BECOMER

LIFE ISN'T MEANT TO BE LIVED PERFECTLY, BUT MERELY TO BE LIVED. BOLDLY, WILDLY, BEAUTIFULLY, UNCERTAINLY, MAGICALLY, LIVED.

Mandy Hale, the single woman: life, love, and a dash of sass

SQUEEZING LIFE

My parenting

My friendships

My relationship

My fun times

I give those my ALL

I enjoy being around people

I love making my family and friends laugh

I enjoy clubbing & dancing

Life to me is like a Big ole orange

And everyday I squeeze the life out of it

You know why???

Because I don't know what tomorrow holds for me so I squeeze the juice out of everyday given to me.

I'm squeezing life for every ounce of juice it can give me

THE ONE THING YOU HAVE THAT NOBODY HAS IS YOU. YOUR VOICE, YOUR MIND, YOUR STORY, YOUR VISION. SO WRITE AND DRAW AND BUILD AND PLAY AND DANCE. LIVE ONLY AS "YOU" CAN.

hplyrikz.com

WISDOM
IT'S SO EXPENSIVE

You've heard the old saying;
Bought sense is better than told

What it really means is if you don't listen to wisdom, You will have to buy it with a life lesson.

BABY… let me tell you from experience I don't care how much money you have, Wisdom is so expensive.

You will go broke buying her and buying her is painful. Buying her will break your heart, your spirit, your will and sometimes your mind.

Buying takes away your time. Buying Wisdom is NO JOKE; it's so expensive buying her but when you buy her, No ONE can steal her from you because you bought that lesson with blood, sweat and a lot of tears.

I bought a few and went bankrupt in the process. I've decided not to be so hardheaded and listen to Wisdom.

Because buying
her…

IT'S SOOO EXPENSIVE!!!

IT'S OKAY IF PEOPLE DON'T LIKE YOU...
MOST PEOPLE DON'T EVEN LIKE THEMSELVES.

NORMAL

Maybe it's just me but I think "normal" is so overrated.

I'm not sure that it is understood that my normal may not be another person's normal.
After all, we are all unique right?

So why do I have to fit into the nice, neat, normal box?

It's just not going to work

Let's face it, normal is so boring and it's almost like I'm a follower of some person who determined what normal should look like probably decades ago.

I'm way too bossy to follow the leader in this normal box that everyone wants me in.

Plus my normal is way more fun and it looks good on me.

Inspired by BEP

IF WE ARE NO LONGER ABLE TO CHANGE THE SITUATION, WE ARE CHALLENGED TO CHANGE OURSELVES.

Victor E Frankl

SWISS CHEESE

Me, insecure? NEVER THAT!!!
Girl come to find out.
Yes me, with my fine, sexy, independent self.
It happened in little segments of my life that I didn't even see at first.
My 1st real boyfriend when I was in high school cheated on me. My daughter's father had another girl pregnant while I was pregnant. Now that hurt me to my core.
Ok, so that's about 3 or 4 holes in the cheese.
Little did I know that I had holes in my security level that was like a slice of Swiss cheese.
I think in the back of my mind, I thought that there must be something wrong with guys, that they can't be loyal.
I was that chick who broke the codes to my dude's phone to check his texts.
It took my Mom to check me on my behavior and I was mad at her but I realized… I was Swiss cheese,
I had holes everywhere!
I needed to take a break from a relationship and totally love me again because I was kinda messed up.
The self-time helped me learn some things.
I realized that what a dude did to me didn't define who I was. I had to stop depositing other people's flaws into my investments because it was creating a deficit in my account
The reality was that I needed to make better choices in who I allowed to choose me.
They may choose me, however, I had to intentionally decide to be chosen.
So no more insecure Swiss cheese holes in my character, at least not when it comes to relationships.
We all have Swiss cheese areas in our lives (that's why some slices have more holes than others)
Some holes, only GOD can helps us fill and some holes, He lets us keep so that we don't get too prideful
Yes, we all have insecurities… We all have Swiss cheese, whether we admit it or not.

LOVE IS NO ASSIGNMENT FOR THE COWARDS

Ovid

I STILL LOVE YOU

We talked all the time
Now not as much
Yet I still love you.

I didn't do things the way you thought
I should And you didn't do things the
way I thought you should.

Yet you are mine and I still love you.

This hurts because I miss talking to
you
I miss us.

But somehow I know that we will get
back to us again...

Because I still love you and I know you
love me too.

ATTRACT WHAT YOU EXPECT, REFLECT WHAT YOU DESIRE, BECOME WHAT YOU RESPECT, MIRROR WHAT YOU ADMIRE .

YOUR CIRCLE

Even though we are young, we have to choose the right circle. A circle is always connected so choose solid people for your circle.
People who will always have your back, people who are not afraid to push you when you get stuck, people who don't run when the thin gets thinner.

What this means is that your circle should love you regardless and ALWAYS squeeze the best out of you even if it's difficult to get your cooperation.

You have to be intentional about your circle and don't take in strays - some people need to stay in the outer court.

So... take a look...
What does you circle look like?

BECOME SO CONFIDENT IN WHO YOU ARE THAT NO ONE'S OPINION OR REJECTION CAN ROCK YOU.

Amazingmemovement.com

I'M NOT GOING TO APOLOGIZE

So there are different breeds of dogs. Each breed has their own characteristics and traits. They didn't create the traits tied to their breed; it's how they were born.

A Chihuahua can't help that it's small, A Poodle can't help that it's hairy and neither can a Pit Bull help that it's strong, determined and resourceful.

So listen, I'm not going to apologize for being a Pit Bull, It is what it is. My personality started in the womb. I came out with the DNA that gradually developed into who I am today.

If you like Chihuahuas or Poodles, then that's probably who you should surround yourself with. Don't come around me and want me to change so you can be comfortable. I'm a Pit and I'm not apologizing for it.

If you don't like Pits, move around because I'm not going to apologize for my DNA

INSPIRED BY JFH

PEACE COMES FROM WITHIN...

DON'T SEEK IT WITHOUT.

Gautama Buddha

ARE YOU SINGLE?

I wasn't always single and I have never been married.
Single means not divided.
Life has a way of breaking you up sometimes
I was broken
I was in pieces, at one time,
I was divided

Single for me has nothing to do with not being married.

Single means that I'm whole,
I'm one,
I'm 100%,
I'm not divided, not broken into pieces

I learned to fall in love with myself then I gathered the pieces of me and put me back together

THEN I BECAME SINGLE

If I ever get married, he will be my better whole not my better half because I am whole so he needs to be too!!!

"

WHENEVER YOU FEEL LIKE GIVING UP, JUST REMEMBER WHY YOU'VE HELD ON FOR SO LONG.

"

THE PROCESS

At times, I have questioned why things that have happened in life happened the way they did. Now I realize that you can't reach your purpose without going through the process.

There is a different process to make buttermilk than there is to make butter.

Because we all have a different purpose, We all have a different process.

The process is not always comfortable, yet it fulfills our purpose.

Be thankful for your process because you may not be able to handle mine.

THE ONLY PEOPLE THAT ARE WORTHY TO BE IN YOUR LIFE ARE THE ONES THAT HELP YOU THROUGH THE BAD TIMES AND LAUGH WITH YOU AFTER THE BAD TIMES PASS.

ARE YOU A SOFA

When I enter my home I see my living room set, My dining room set, I see my bedroom set.

Everything is present Physically.

We need to learn the difference between physical   presence   and   emotional presence.

I work on being emotionally present for my Babies
Not just at home for my Babies.

In my relationship, I work on being emotionally   present,   Not   just physically with him.

We can't brag about our presence in people's lives if all we are is a sofa

Are you present emotionally or just physically?

Are you a SOFA???

WHEN YOU CAN'T CONTROL WHAT'S HAPPENING, CHALLENGE YOURSELF TO CONTROL THE WAY YOU RESPOND TO WHAT'S HAPPENING.
THAT'S WHERE YOUR POWER IS.

Sun-gazing.com

CHALLENGES

You ever started watching a football game and couldn't finish seeing the game so you recorded it?

You didn't want to know the end results because you wanted to see it for yourself but you knew that somehow you were going to hear the score before you were able to see it for yourself.

That's kind of how we need to face our challenges. The difference is we need to set our mind to already know the outcome. Regardless of what challenges we face. There is already deposited in us the ability to overcome those challenges. Overcoming challenges does not always mean that we defeat the challenge. Sometimes we just learn from our challenge to prepare for the next one.

The thing is, if the challenges don't take us out then we are still victorious.

Learn not to fear challenges. Just set your mind towards an expected outcome that you will either defeat or learn from your challenges.

"

THERE COMES A TIME TO STOP TRYING TO MAKE THINGS RIGHT WITH PEOPLE THAT WON'T OWN THEIR PART IN WHAT WENT WRONG.

"

I HEARD YOU

You say that because I grew up in a single family home I'm more likely to drop out of school. I heard you but I really didn't hear you.
You say that I will probably live in the lower income areas of the city. I heard you but I really didn't hear you

You say that the likelihood of me handling myself properly in a corporate setting is slim. I heard you but I really didn't hear you.

You know why I really didn't hear you?
I grew up in a single family home by a woman who grew up in a single family home and she has 2 degrees and working on a 3rd. Neither she nor I grew up in low income areas and That Lady wouldn't let me drop out of school even if I tried my best to do so. She pushed me to go to college and made me work in a law firm for my summer jobs when I was old enough to work.
I speak and interview well, I'm intelligent and my children will be too.

So yeah... I heard you but I really didn't hear you

"

JUST BECAUSE SOME PEOPLE ARE FUELED BY DRAMA DOESN'T MEAN YOU HAVE TO ATTEND THE PERFORMANCE.

"

SO WHY YOU CRYING???

Ok, Ok, Ok, so he said he doesn't want to be with you anymore?
And he told you that you got too much going on and he ain't got time for that?
Oh, he told you that you're not gonna find another dude like him?
And what… you're gonna be lonely???
Ok friend, but why are you crying?
If the dude can't stand by your side when the thin gets thinner, then he needs to leave and hopefully you won't have to be bothered with another dude like that!
You free now!!!
Please tell me you are not letting what he said define who you are because there is a man out there that can make you feel like your lowest valleys are mountain tops,
A man that has made up in his mind that there is no place he would rather be than with you regardless of the ups and downs
This is your time to redefine who you are
But first, you have to take some time and fall in love with yourself again.
Once you fall in love with yourself, loneliness won't be a problem because you will enjoy your own company.
So why you crying?
Girl now you are free to nurture your most valuable player YOU!!!
SO STOP CRYING; YOU GOT WORK TO DO.

ON AVERAGE, NEARLY 20 PEOPLE PER MINUTE ARE PHYSICALLY ABUSED BY AN INTIMATE PARTNER IN THE UNITED STATES. DURING ONE YEAR, THIS EQUATES TO MORE THAN 10 MILLION WOMEN AND MEN.

NATIONAL STATISTICS

MINDING OUR BUSINESS

My friend and I heard them fight all the time.

Whenever I visited on the weekend, it was a guarantee to hear them fighting.
You know how it is, we live in the Chi and you mind your business and hope people mind theirs.

The thing is, sometimes minding your business can do more harm than good.

So my friend and I were chillin and there they go again.

Just shaking our heads and minding our business, Only this time, it was different... Someone got KILLED.
This time it was different.

Domestic Violence just got REAL
This time it was different while we were minding our business.

IF YOU CAN DREAM IT, YOU CAN DO IT.

Walt Disney

I DON'T ALWAYS GET IT RIGHT

I started out with some plans on how I was going to get it together. Turning 27 years old with 2 children and hadn't really decided what I wanted to be when I grew up was not part of the plan.

You know, I'm still young, yet I feel like I don't have a lot of time which is crazy… maybe because I lost my Baby Girl's daddy and life just doesn't seem like you can trust it anymore. I have a lot of "what ifs" going through my head yet I know that I've made some good choices; it's just that the bad ones cost so much!!!

I don't always get it right yet I never give up trying because I'm stubborn like that. You know if we look at ourselves for real and just be honest, we know the things that we need to change to be better. The problem is we like those things that can be problems because we think we have super hero status and can conquer the problem. Well, I realize that I'm not a real good super hero and I don't get it right a lot of times. The thing is I'm willing to face reality and do better this time… after all, this thing called life just got real!!!

"

TWO THINGS DEFINE YOU:

YOUR PATIENCE WHEN YOU HAVE NOTHING, AND YOUR ATTITUDE WHEN YOU HAVE EVERYTHING.

"

GETTING TO KNOW ME

People in relationships are always talking about knowing their mate.

I'm still getting to know my damn self I guess because I'm young, I'm evolving into who I'm gonna be later.

Sometimes, I do stupid stuff and then sometimes I amaze myself and handle a situation with so much maturity that I have to look at myself.

I'm trying to get to a place where I'm consistent with the maturity thing. However, it's more fun doing the opposite.

It's cool though, watching me grow into a better woman.

I'm really paying attention to my actions. I'm getting to know me and the whys that make me, me.

IF YOU CHANGE NOTHING ,

NOTHING WILL CHANGE.

WHAT'S THE TAKE AWAY FROM THIS?

I get it, whether good or bad, there is a lesson in all things.
Ok… but COVID 19!!!

People dying by the tens of thousands.
The whole country on lock-down

What am I supposed to learn from this???

Death and isolation really puts things in perspective. I have spent time with people that were a waste of my time. I'm realizing that tomorrow is really not guaranteed!!!

Am I working on being the best me that I can be??? Not really… I haven't given life my best. I've taken time for granted.

My take away from this is:
Make the best of every minute that God gives me.

Don't be selfish with the blessings that I have been given.

And most of all, be thankful for the good as well as the bad because if I made it through then there is still a purpose for my life.

DON'T MISTAKE SILENCE FOR WEAKNESS.
SMART PEOPLE DON'T MAKE BIG MOVES OUT LOUD.

thegoodvibes.co

FRAME YOUR FUTURE

When you are starting a business you have to write a business plan.

You project your estimated future profits

You strive to meet those goals

Shouldn't you frame your future for your personal life also?

When we are young, we are so care free and we don't realize that time can go by so fast.

It's almost like we think time will stop for us until we get it together.

Well it doesn't!

Yeah we can still kick it, but we need to frame our future so that time doesn't catch us slipping.

Framing our future gives us guidelines and timelines to work toward.

Yeah we're still young but we got to frame our future because young don't last forever

"

YOU NEED TO STOP DOING THINGS FOR SOMEONE WHEN YOU FIND OUT THAT IT'S EXPECTED RATHER THAN APPRECIATED.

"

I LET YOU CHOOSE ME

Dude, let me help you get this relationship thing straight.
Sure, the Bible says that a man who finds a wife finds a good thing, however, I made the decision to let you keep me.

This whole possession thing you got going on is an illusion. I own all of me and I made the choice to let you enter into a lease agreement with me. Every time
I walk out of the door, all of me goes with me because I own me.

I let you choose me; I'm the gift, you aren't.

God put Adam to sleep to give him a surprise, WOMAN, which is why the Bible says "find a wife" because a good woman is a hidden treasure.

I'm the prize in this relationship not you so stop treating me like property that you possess.

Yes, you chose me, however, I had the final say and I LET YOU CHOOSE ME.

MATTHEW 6:33 KING JAMES VERSION (KJV)

BUT SEEK YE FIRST THE KINGDOM OF GOD, AND HIS RIGHTEOUSNESS; AND ALL THESE THINGS SHALL BE ADDED UNTO YOU.

THE MANUFACTURER

Most things in life depend on our choices
If you have an old inexpensive car and you need parts you
probably will choose not to buy a manufacturer's part
The middle man is who we depend on most in this society
We don't farm or own cattle and chickens so the grocery stores are our middle man. However the manufacturer is essential for some things in order for them to function properly. It is strongly advised to use manufacturer parts for a Mercedes or Maserati. The same holds true for all our needs. God is the source for all our needs, He is the Manufacturer. After all, everything that we receive is a resource from the main source.
If we go to the grocery store to buy oranges the grocery store is the resource from the orange farmers who are the main source. So why do we think our job is our source instead of a resource from God. Have you ever been unemployed yet still survived through another resource.
Your education is a resource because if God the creator had not wired you with the ability to retain information you would not have accomplished your degree(s).
Even your gifts and abilities come from the Manufacturer
If he wants to shut you down he can. Don't put a lot of stock in the middle men in your lives; They are only resources I put my stock in the Manufacturer because God creates all my resources

THE SECRET TO GETTING AHEAD IS GETTING STARTED.

THIS IS NOT A DRILL

I didn't listen right away…

Girl I was thinking I had plenty of time to get serious about life. Next thing I know, I'm 25 years old and still experimenting with life.

I woke up one morning and said "I'm heading to my 30's!!!" I realized that this is not a drill and that I needed to get it together.

Time is just doing what it does so I needed to start living life with a goal and purpose.

My girls and I have been clubbing and kickin' it; buying new outfits to go out and not putting $$$ in a savings account.

Where oh where did the years go? Life just got real…

THIS IS NOT A DRILL

LIFE IS WHAT HAPPENS TO YOU WHILE YOU'RE BUSY MAKING OTHER PLANS.

Allen Sanders.

THIS WAS NOT THE PLAN

So we talked on the phone this morning and I sent you a pic of our baby all dressed up for a special day at school. Then I dropped the Girls off at school and I went to school.
All day I was thinking about what you said.
You want to settle down, buy a
couple of buildings and get out of the game.

WOW! You even asked me if I would marry you and get past the wrongs you've done to hurt me.

After thinking about it all day, my plan was to wait and see if you were serious.

Then I get the call…
You've been shot and you might not make it.

OH GOD NO!!!

This was not the plan.

I love you...
I'll marry you...
Just LIVE!

Menace, JUST LIVE... don't die.

"

I'M SELFISH, IMPATIENT, AND A LITTLE INSECURE.
I MAKE MISTAKES, I'M OUT OF CONTROL, AND SOMETIMES, HARD TO HANDLE. BUT IF YOU CAN'T HANDLE ME AT MY WORST, THEN YOU SURE AS HELL DON'T DESERVE ME AT MY BEST.

Marilyn Monroe

"

HOW I'M WIRED

My Mom always says "Everything ain't for everybody." I get it because the way I'm wired, sensitive people ain't for me.

Their feelings would always be hurt and it wouldn't be intentional. It's just that I'm not good with softness. My crew needs to be strong. They have to be able to handle the blows of life verbally and otherwise, they need to be able to stand some stuff without taking everything to heart.

It's just the way I'm wired.

I'm not good with soft.

Because I'm wired tough. I'm wired strong.

I'm wired to take a blow and give one back.

It's just how I'm wired.

BECAUSE OF YOU,

I LAUGH HARDER,
CRY A LITTLE LESS
&
SMILE A LOT MORE.

THAT LADY

That Lady gets on my LAST NERVE and I'm sure I get on her's too.

She is always in my business, although most times I need her to be.

I get so mad at her that I don't want to speak to her again but that doesn't last long because it helps when I talk to her.

I know That Lady loves me and I love her too.

I wouldn't be here without her and regardless of what I say when I'm mad,

That Lady is my Mom and nobody else can say anything about her!!!

SPONSORSHIP CAN COME TO YOU IN DIFFERENT WAYS. YOU NEVER KNOW WHO IS WATCHING YOU. SO BE SPONSOR-READY AT ALL TIMES .

Millette Granville

SPONSORSHIP

Folks can talk all they want, but everybody, (men and women) needs a sponsor at some point in life.

Businesses seek sponsorship so that they do not have to deplete their assets by carrying the load alone.

Some events are only successful due to sponsorship.

Politicians have sponsors so why can't I have a sponsor to advance my needs and desires?

Trust me sponsorship has it's perks.

" —

SHOW RESPECT TO PEOPLE WHO DON'T DESERVE IT; NOT AS A REFLECTION OF THEIR CHARACTER BUT AS A REFLECTION OF YOURS.

Dave Willis

"

IF YOU KNEW WHAT I WAS THINKING

Everybody talks about keeping it 100.
Trust me that's not what they mean. You know how I know? Because I tried it.

I was raw out of my mouth - whatever came up came out. Guess what? It was a mess! I was talked about, disliked, and frowned upon.

So now... I get it. Society wants the decaf version of keeping it 100 with some sugar added. So now I say a little bit mixed with some sugar and cream, because
let's face it, I'm not decaf; I put on my dynamic smile then give them 50% and keep it moving. I do this cause I have babies to raise and keeping it 100 in society doesn't put food on the table.

So yeah, I may candy coat some stuff to provide for my babies...

BUT...

If you knew what I was thinking.

NOT EVERY THING THAT'S FACED CAN BE CHANGED-BUT NOTHING CAN BE CHANGED UNTIL IT'S FACED.

James Baldwin

REST

Adulthood is so overrated.
Remember as a shorty, all you had to do was clean your room and a few other chores.
Man, then you could play and do your thing, just resting; knowing that your parents (for me it was just my Mom) would take care of the rest.
We couldn't wait to be grown and do what we wanted to do when
we wanted to do it.
NEWS FLASH!!! Most times, I don't want to go to work, I don't always want to drive the speed limit. I truly don't want to spend most of my money on bills
But you know what; I discovered how to rest again like I did when I was a shorty.
I REST in GOD now
After all, I'm not really in control anyway so I might as well just do my chores and let GOD handle the rest.
I trusted my Mom and he made her so I know I can trust him to cover me when I have no clue how to cover myself.
Man, it feels good to REST again!!!

THE QUESTION ISN'T WHO'S GOING TO LET ME; IT'S WHO'S GOING TO STOP ME?

Ayn Rand

MAN CHILD

I knew this pregnancy was different. I felt different. I had more strength and energy. Confidence was my default mode. Then I found out why... I was carrying a man child

A KING

He made my hair grow (as if I needed that) and my skin glowed much more than with the Girls.

His kicks and elbows were strong.

My man child was my only full term birth.
He was determined to have it all together when he came out of the gate.

He came out looking strong and in charge.

My man child.

I gave birth to a MAN CHILD

"

IF THERE COMES A DAY WHERE WE CAN'T BE TOGETHER, KEEP ME IN YOUR HEART, I'LL STAY THERE FOREVER.

"

WE'VE BEEN THERE

This thing is like Magic
Regardless of how old we get
Or who we are with, Our bond is never broken

I move out of town,
You get another baby,
I have a baby.

And still, you've been there.

We get mad, But still
you've been there.

You are the only guy that I consider my Best
Friend because you've been there.

We can talk about everything because we've
been together through everything.

I get on your nerves and you get on mine.

And still,
you've been there

You even call my Mother "Ma".
Cuz you've been there

I'm thankful that for over 16 years We've
been there for each other.

Boi I love you to the moon and back.

CUZ WE'VE BEEN THERE

PUSH YOUR BOUNDARIES...

THAT'S WHAT

THEY ARE THERE FOR.

COMPETITION

Talking about competitive, that's me.
Comparing myself, striving to be better
than the rest... all of that.

The only difference is that I'm in
competition with yesterday's me.
I'm not competing with NOBODY ELSE because
I don't want to be like ANYBODY ELSE.

I love myself some me. I just want to be a
better me than yesterday. So, if the meal I
cooked for my babies yesterday was
slammin', then today I have to outdo
myself.

If my last presentation in class was an
"A", then I'm pushing for an "A+" the next
time.

The reality is that I may not make the mark
everyday but I'm always in competition.

YES I'm real competitive, It's just that
I'm competitive with my MVP; me.

IT IS BETTER TO BE HATED FOR WHAT YOU ARE, THAN TO BE LOVED FOR WHAT YOU ARE NOT.

Andre Girde, Autumn Leaves

PERSONAL REPRESENTATIVE

I just laugh when people who have been around me for a period of time and are so shocked when they finally meet me. The thing is they were interacting with my personal representative.

Let me tell you, my personal representative is the bomb she displays the diplomatic, polite, sweet part of me at all times. My personal representative goes to interviews, meetings, doctor's appointment, business interactions, my babies' school, etc.
I even have her go on the first few dates with a new guy or when I meet new people and potential friends.

Now let's face it. At some point, some people are going to have to meet the whole me… I don't understand the shock and confusion. Doesn't everyone have a personal representative?
I believe that everyone has or should have a personal representative, especially since everyone and I mean everyone has an unfiltered side to them. So stop being so shocked when a person's personal representative leaves the room.

NOW THE REAL FUN BEGINS

INSPIRED BY SRG

"PEOPLE WILL FORGET WHAT YOU SAID,
PEOPLE WILL FORGET WHAT YOU DID,
BUT PEOPLE WILL NEVER FORGET HOW YOU MADE THEM FEEL

Maya Angelou

DO A SERVICE TO YOUR CHILDREN

Your children are not your slaves.
We as parents should treat them in the way
that we want them to become; Thoughtful,
considerate, and polite.

Do a service to your children by verbally
expressing your gratitude and love for what
you ask and expect of them.

When asking them to get you a glass of
water, say please and thank you.
Tell them you love them. Even though you
show it, say it!!!

Teach them by example how to verbally
express positive feelings and emotions.
We show anger and displeasure so why not do
a service to our children and show positive
things like "I love you", "You did a great
job today", "I'm proud of you", "Sleep
well", "Have good dreams".

Do a service to your children because they
may have to service you when you get old.

TRUST YOURSELF, YOU KNOW MORE THAN YOU THINK YOU DO.

Benjamin Spock

ACCEPT THE GOOD

Look, I know you have been through a lot in relationships.

Yeah, you have suffered a lot of pain and made poor choices.
Yet that doesn't mean that those things are your destiny!!!

Girl, accept the good that has come into your life and stop waiting for the other shoe to drop. Maybe the other shoe landed in somebody else's yard.

Life is short. He cares about you, he is paying attention to your needs, and you are scared because he is better to you than you have ever had?

Girl, you better stop being scared and accept the good before I hurt you myself!!!

I KNOW HOW I LOOK NOW

It's like going to a poor area of Chicago
You see abandon buildings and low income housing...
People hanging out on corners, Loud music and no peace.

It's hard to see beyond that when it's all in your face.

Same with me...
Single mother of 3 children...

In my late 20's, Went to college but didn't finish...
No real career goals yet.

I know how that looks...

Yet, just like Chicago,
There's more to the City than the Hood.

Chicago's skyline is AMAZING!!!
And you can see it from the Hood.

You just have to look beyond what's in your face

Look beyond my single parent status and my present situation. You gotta keep watching because even if I don't impress you, my Babies will.

My Babies are me and I pour all that I didn't do and should have done into them.

The things I didn't listen to I make sure they listen.

My Babies are Chicago's Beautiful Skyline. They are the best part of me.

So stop looking at what's in your face

Look beyond
I KNOW HOW I LOOK NOW...BUT KEEP WATCHING

ACKNOWLEGDMENTS

I give all honor and praise to Almighty God, for without him I would not have been sane, much less able to accomplish this book.
To my niece Sonja, I thank you for all the assistance that you provided in finding people/sources to help me complete this journey. Then there is Shiesha who was such an inspiration. When I slowed down with my writing she pushed me with words of encouragement.

To Tiwan & Sabrina for assisting in caring for my Grands upon their arrival to Florida and Tiesha for taking care of the Girls hair.

Also, Dr. Lusharon Wiley who has been a Godsend. Her support over the past couple of years has been unbelievable.

To my segregate daughters Della Reese & Kirsten you two have been so helpful in taking on the task of Auntie when you both did not have to after my Baby transitioned. You both have shown that friendship surpasses life here on earth.

I am so thankful to so many others who have been supportive so please know that if your name is not mentioned, it is because there is not enough space here to mention all of the amazing people in my life whom are loved and appreciated by myself and my Grands.

ACKNOWLEGDMENTS

I give all honor and praise to Almighty God, for without him I would not have been sane, much less able to accomplish this book. To my niece Sonja, I thank you for all the assistance that you provided in finding people/sources to help me complete this journey. Then there is Shiesha who was such an inspiration. When I slowed down with my writing she pushed me with words of encouragement. Also, Dr. Lusharon Wiley who has been a Godsend. Her support over the past couple of years has been unbelievable.

To my segregate daughters Della Reese & Kirsten you two have been so helpful in taking on the task of Auntie when you both did not have to after my Baby transitioned. You both have shown that friendship surpasses life here on earth.

I am so thankful to so many others who have been supportive so please know that if your name is not mentioned, it is because there is not enough space here to mention all of the amazing in my life whom are loved and appreciated by myself and my Grands.

APPENDIX

Laying in bed doing alot of thinking and trying to find my motivation back its so crazy cause had I would have known everything that I know now my dreams would have been accomplish by now but would I had been happy to the key. Now really know I just need to work on my happiness now. I love the woman I'm becoming I'm more in tune with myself wisdom certainly comes with age I know Im a bad bitch I'm very secure and want to empower my girls to know they are beautiful and know their worth

I promise if I knew
the things that I
know now back when
I was 14 my life
would be a whole lot
smoother and better
but my goal is to
have a strong finish
I first need to ~~xxxxx~~
~~xxxxx~~ single certain ppl
out my life for a
while. ~~xxxxxxxxxxxxxx~~
~~xxxxxxxxxxxxxxxxxxx~~

Always remember you are BRAVER
than you believe STRONGER Than you
seem And SMARTER Than you think ●

Your procrastination
from Yesterday is
not my emergency
today.
Koda

I been in a real funky mood and need to snap back real quick. I thought I was going to be stressing and gaining anxiety with all the classes but actually its not all that bad. I will be done with everything before the summer when I start. I have a lot going on but I want to learn something out of it. I want to change from this. I dont want to make the same mistakes any more. I need to learn from these so I can elevate to the next level. I have to get things in order and make things right. I'm so hard on myself and dont give myself enough credit. I wont to ~~instill~~ instill so much in my kids I need to focus more on Zia Cathy inspire me so much as a parent thats how I wont to be I always think of what I could do that giving and helping my children.

You dont always need a plan.
Sometimes you just need to breathe, trust, let go + see what happens
        - Mandy Hale